E. MO

Moncure, Jane Belk

Word Bird's
Halloween words

$11.93

DATE			
MY 19 '89	JE 8 '90	AG 13 '91	NO 28 '92
JE 27 '89	JE 28 '90	SE 9 '91	MY 3 '93
JY 20 '89	JY 13 '90	SE 30 '91	MY 27 '93
AG 9 '89	AG 7 '90	SE 30 '91	JY 1 '93
OC 16 '89	OC 11 '90	OC 20 '91	JY 27 '93
	FE 5 '91	OC 20 '91	OC 1 '93
NO 2 '89	MR 16 '91		
NO 28 '89	AP 15 '91	FE 28 '92	OC 19 '93
FE 2 '90	JE 6 '91	MY 27 '92	NO 8 '93
MR 1 '90	JY 6 '91	JY 2 '92	JUL 14 '99
MR 15 '90	JY 22 '91	OC 12 '92	OCT 17 '94
AP 12 '90		OC 26 '92	NOV 25 '94 '95

JUL 26 '96'

JAN 10 '97

WORD BIRD'S
HALLOWEEN WORDS

by Jane Belk Moncure
illustrated by Vera Gohman

Created by

THE CHILD'S WORLD

Distributed by CHILDRENS PRESS ®
Chicago, Illinois

CHILDRENS PRESS HARDCOVER EDITION
ISBN 0-516-06576-9

CHILDRENS PRESS PAPERBACK EDITION
ISBN 0-516-46576-7

Library of Congress Cataloging in Publication Data

Moncure, Jane Belk.
  Word Bird's Halloween words.

  (Word house words for early birds)
  Summary: Word Bird puts words about Halloween in
his word house, introducing such words as "witches,"
"costumes," and "masks."
    1. Vocabulary—Juvenile literature.   2. Halloween—
Juvenile literature.   [1. Halloween.   2. Vocabulary]
I. Gohman, Vera Kennedy, 1922-   ill.   II. Title.
III. Series: Moncure, Jane Belk.   Word house words for
early birds.
PE1449.M529   1987   428.1   86-31024
ISBN 0-89565-359-1

1 2 3 4 5 6 7 8 9 10 11 12 R 95 94 93 92 91 90 89 88 87

WORD BIRD'S
HALLOWEEN WORDS

Word Bird made a...

word house.

"I will put Halloween
words in my house,"
he said.

He put in these words—

Halloween

October 31

pumpkin patch

jack-o'-lantern

orange

black

Halloween colors

black cats

witches

13

brooms

scarecrow

bats

haunted house

spooks

"Boo."

owls

"Who-oo-o."

masks

monsters

costumes

parade

Halloween party

safety bug

"Trick or treat."

Halloween

witches

OCTOBER

October 31

brooms

pumpkin patch

scarecrow

jack-o'-lantern

bats

Halloween colors

haunted house

black cats

30

Halloween words with

Word Bird ?

spooks

"Boo."

owls

"Who-oo-o."

masks

monsters

costumes

parade

Halloween party

safety bug

"Trick or treat."

You can make a Halloween word house. You can put Word Bird's words in your house and read them too.

Can you think of other Halloween words to put in your word house?